Beautiful Monsters

Also by Jeffrey Greene

Poetry:

American Spirituals
To the Left of the Worshiper
Glimpses of the Invisible World in New Haven (chapbook)

Memoir:

French Spirits

Nature:

The Golden-Bristled Boar
Water from Stone: The Story of Selah, Bamberger Ranch
Reserve

Beautiful Monsters

Poems by Jeffrey Greene

Nov. 9 2010 NYC

For Catherine —

*A great joy and
honor to serve with you
on the Mirror Visions
board and to share
the pleasure of so
many concerts.
Very warmly*

Pecan Grove Press   San Antonio, Texas

Cover art: "The Wolf of Gubbio" (1877) by Luc-Oliver Merson

ISBN: 978-1-931247-77-1

Pecan Grove Press
Box AL
1 Camino Santa Maria
San Antonio, TX 78228

Grateful acknowledgment is made to the following publications:

Agni Review: "Beautiful Monsters"

The Alaska Quarterly: "The Satellite Dish at La Quinta Inn"

Anna Davidson Rosenberg Award: "Timepiece (III)"

The Café Review: "Vengeance"

The Crab Orchard Review: "The Last Tiger in Singapore"

The Greensboro Review: "Virginia," "A Condensed History with Wolves"

Her Royal Majesty: "The Mole"

The Los Angeles Review: "Quiet Storm"

The Nation: "Evening Ferry" published as "Charlestown"

North American Review: "Electric Boat Corporation"

Notre Dame Review: "The Evening's Theme," "Comments on 'O-Magnet-South'"

Paris/Atlantic: "Timepiece (III)"

Ploughshares: "Extended Night," "Bath of Yellow Light"

Poetry Northwest: "On Marriage"

Poetry: "Beginnings"

The Sewanee Review: "Ministering Spirits," "Château de Chambord," "The Meeting," "Greensboro"

Solo: "The Weather Channel"

The Southern California Anthology: "Your Lingual Hearts"

Southern Poetry Review: "Aeneas in Houston," "Whitman at Falmouth"

The Southern Review: "An Untruth"

The Southwest Review: "The Mayor's Daughter," "Elegy for a Muse"

Upstairs at Duroc: "Carthage," "Timepiece (I)"

Reprint: "Beginnings" in *Poetry Daily*; "The Evening's Theme" in *Notre Dame Review Anthology*

Work on this book was supported by fellowships from the National Endowment for the Arts, The Vermont Studio Center, and Château de Lavigny International Writers' Residence.

My deepest gratitude to Charles Siebert, Melanie Almeder, Bex Brian, Tobé Malawista (and Mirror Visions), Renée Harlow, Michelle Boisseau, Tom & Randy Cobb, Cecilia Woloch, Heather Hartley, Laura Strachan, William Olsen, Tricia Barker, Laura Hendrie and Mary McFadden for their support and literary collaboration.

I am especially indebted to Susan Prospere, who contributed to each of these poems.

For Mary
And for Stephen E. Malawista, M.D.

Table of Contents

1.

Beautiful Monsters

It is said the gods gave us the boar
to keep us from eating each other.

1

Robinson Jeffers called them beautiful monsters,
naked knives in their jaws, black-maned,
bristling in midnight bushes, tusking the earth
while stars turned downward
into the Pacific.

Nations had fallen
in the Old World, but it wasn't our affair
according to Jeffers. He wrote of ridges over the sea,
freedom, and the Old World boars,

escapees in the Santa Lucia hills
in the chilly mists of paradise.

2

The purer ones
fled the hunting reserve, Palo Corona,
to invade the Randolph Hearst Ranch
and range as far as Carmel Point and Tor,
the house Jeffers built from sea stones.

The boars mixed with feral swine
the Spanish brought to their missions

and those that wandered off from pioneer settlements.
I have seen them myself, black on black
night on the banks of the Big Sur.

3

Conquistador Hernando de Soto brought them to the South
from Florida to Arkansas, horses and guns
moving in a swarm of pigs. De Soto died in a fever
in the "razorback" state, his body
sunken in the Mississippi.

La Salle brought swine
to Matagorda, Texas, stalked by the fierce
Karankawas slathered in alligator grease.

His own men killed him—
not his first mutiny since claiming
the heartland for the French.

4

The English, Irish, Germans,
and Scandinavians brought pigs to America,
free-range foraging, reproducing madly,
butchered in the cold season,
hogs and hominy to feed the slaves.

They mixed with boars in the Great Smokies,
offspring with long snouts,
coarse bristles down the spine,
and straight tails with a gnarled tuft.

                                                  They are
their own tribe, a strict society in motion,
sharing the terrain with us,
awakening at dusk and flourishing
impossibly obscure.

                     5

                    If Jeffers could see
his beautiful monsters now,
he'd think it a war
we were losing by numbers,

                                 despite
Kalashnikovs from helicopters,
the dawg-hawg rodeos,
the *naked knives in their jaws* cut with a bolt cutter,
pit bulls pinning them in seconds in the soft
charcoal smoke of the fairgrounds,

and the knife hunter,
"hunting on the brink of sanity."

6

Hung from a tree, the human-sized body
is split, the heart branched
to the lungs like ours.

We replace our damaged
valves with theirs, fit their bones to our bones,
their skin over our burns,
their hormones for our disease . . .

inject our stem cells into their embryos,
their entrails have our stench,
beautiful monsters of our own making.

2.

The Evening's Theme

for Jack Gilbert

Let's say it's toward the end of evening in a small town
in New England, with early November breezes and friends,

where the dinner discussion turns to a theme. Let's say
this time it's heroes, appropriate for poets over wine and stew,

but the definitions get stickier as they always do, ranging
from small acts of human decency to mythic figures at the ends

of their journeys, and only what lies between gets interesting,
those lucky lunacies that changed the world, Copernican

or Lutheran, the unveering will of Magellan, down through
gradient heroes that make a nation and keep it dangerous,

until we are down to our own fathers, who must bear the heroic
flaws of our expectations. Then the discussion finally goes

to the hypothetical and from there to hell, where we
could start over with weaknesses. We shift to places

where we grew up: bridges in Pittsburgh
or parishes in Wales or Raminski's daughter whom I thought

so brave to touch my brother and me near a coal bin.
I think of our landlord Raminski, the day he caught fire

burning paint off our building and pouring fuel on a lit pilot.
My brother cut his clothes off while blistering his own hands.

I know that it qualifies only as an act of human decency.
Still my brother, only a kid, looked mythic

with a carbon steel knife and Raminski sitting in shock
on the beaten earth of the backyard. Not even

my brother's gin or cocaine changes my mind.
Achilles is nothing without Hector.

The Mayor's Daughter

Her handsome father was a renegade
in the city's party,
and a bad politician in the end,
even among his friends.
Too young to vote, I'd canvas
Howard Avenue and Congress,
with a young black Democrat
who could talk his way
through a wall to sign up
the suspicious and the "underprivileged"
where half the houses
are left to ruin now.
I'd drive the voters
to a nearby school,
and I'd wait in the leaf fall
to take them home.
I was dating the mayor's daughter
although *dating* is not the right word
for what we did,
except to say we kissed.
That year Berryman wrote
Love & Fame in two months.
I'd read it a decade later
wondering how he could make
a crushing art of his own name.

Bath of Yellow Light

My aunt sat with a drink,
the afternoon light
on the sill and half

of her beautiful face
when she spoke of
her first death.

It happened after a storm.
Silver rays
formed beams on the sea

through the gray clouds
and the surf pounded
the sandy stretches

of the Jersey shore.
A rip current carried her away.
She struggled and may

have swum parallel
to the beach, I don't know.
But she said

that letting herself go
was the highlight of her life,
going into what

should have been
the end of consciousness,
only it wasn't,

nor was it a return
to the womb,
but something more

like the brain dying
in a bath of yellow light.
You would think

her grateful when saved,
but instead she cried
with anger. My aunt knew

I'd love hearing this story
punctuated by tears
and the soft convulsions

of a woman's grief.
I was fully embraced
in its radiance.

Extended Night

Each drop of rain is a fraction of a second.
It rains all night.
You are nursing your mother,
and you think at night
that you see
what she is made of.
You are so tired
with your eyes open
you dream a curtain
becoming a strip of clear sky
between the branches of trees.
Your mother tries to get out of bed.
Sometimes she is escaping
the fire of years ago
and sometimes she knows
she is dying.
If the rain on one leaf could be heard
it would be the sound
of one life passing.

Electric Boat Corporation

Each year, the winter quarter, I taught
a course at the extension
for students coming off the day shift,
building Ohio-class Trident subs,
which can deliver twenty-four
missiles, each with five warheads.
One year it was the *West Virginia*.
You could see it from the apogee
of the Gold Star Bridge, nosing out
of the pale-green shed of the shipyard.
The students were older. Some had
served on subs and lived undetected
under the world's oceans.
In 1959, my mother came to Groton
and lay down on the long deck
of the *George Washington*
to protest the Polaris missile.
The next year, the *Triton*,
circling the globe without surfacing,
retraced the voyage of Magellan.
Each week I'd look at the *West Virginia*,
and imagine my students welding it,
wiring it, and installing its hydraulics.
Who wouldn't marvel at the technology,
going back to ancient Greek philosophers
who somehow thought of atoms?
In its own way, the long, sleek hull
of the *West Virginia* was beautiful

at the edge of the water. Sometimes
it lived half-visible in the ocean haze,
the most deadly machine the earth
has known. I never asked my students
what they thought of what they made,
nor did they ask me why I write poetry.

Evening Ferry

Thomas Aquinas, Saint Augustine,
and our own angelic doctor:
Reverend Brown,
after dinner and too much bourbon,
assuming we traveled
with him down the road
of philosophical references,
chanting Latin to the earthbound
cottage's thin walls—
the ocean and the bugs
and coastal land of the Indians.
Afterwards, Mary and I walked
the path of crushed
clams and oysters
as if to share the cool
air with the dead and a few
raccoons scouting
the seaweed line along the sand.
Saint Augustine said,
No one hates his body,
but tonight we can hardly
see our own as if they
were ashes tossed
from the evening ferry
or impressions on stone,
markers for the lost at sea.

Timepiece

Once photographers needed
darkness for their art
to manipulate light the way
a glassblower needed fire.
My brother found enough
darkness at the New Haven
Clock Factory where artists
built studios like burrows
in the corners of vacant
assembly rooms. It was
a journey just to find him—
steel doors, locks, and benches;
windows jagged and winter gusts
with snow. As many as 2000
workers worked by the 1920s.
I drank and smoked with my
brother's friends in the 70s
watching a fringe art called video
that made sex as candid as light
turning the camera on ourselves
slowly in this factory that
produced the first jeweled watches,
dashboard clocks, and timed
fuses for warfare. My brother
bartended the Gypsy, did crack,
took self-portraits dressed up

as Mercury in silver on his way
to a party. When he slept, daylight
filled the unheated factory.
I don't know if he thought
these were his best years,
his best art, sleeping with
negatives drying in strips
weighted with clothespins.
One man died in a first-floor fire—
falling into a stupor with
a cigarette—that left my
brother living like a refugee.
The factory is for sale now,
Johnny's Adult Entertainment
at one end and the rest
unchanged, even some tools
left for spring timepieces
when the world was still
buying the electric clock.

3.

Ministering Spirits

What is the resistance to death of the ministering spirits
if not a mission between the sea and the wilderness
in the bare winter woods of New England,

where saints and strangers were starving to death
by twos and threes until half were gone and the rest
lay waiting? Captain Standish tended the fires and defenses

and with Brewster, the Elder, cleaned the filth of grateful patients,
fearless under the peering hatred of the native ghosts
whose stores of colored corn had been raided.

Three Whitman Poems

1. The Meeting

They met just once at the *Broadway Journal's* office,
"The Raven" poet having published Whitman's essay.
Poe charmed him with courtesy and elegance,
which dictated everything about the moment
in which one imagines the engendering of opposites,
an American hybrid, a Hart Crane, but does the gift
ever come from other poets, disgrace, or dark magnetism?
Whitman dismissed Poe's work, "dazzling
but no heat" and in a year Poe was dying,
in poverty, as was his young, consumptive wife.
Whitman recalled him later a victim of history,
dark, quiet, handsome—Southern from top to toe.

2. Comments on "O Magnet-South"

Who else but Whitman could be homesick
for a region where he was not born—
the swamps of Florida, the deep woods
in Tennessee, and the Georgia savannah?
Who else could translocate the love of
birth-things, transparent or growing
or full of tropical odors transported by divinity?
He braved the word *dear*, meaning
both beloved and costly, a word
as magnetic as north and south,
sympathetic as the poet's two birds,
the thrush's pure notes at the edge of night
and the mockingbird—*the American mimic*.

3. Whitman at Falmouth

A star of shrapnel tore George's cheek
in the pretty smoke of artillery
which was no longer pretty
after Bull Run, Antietam, and defeat
with Burnside at Fredericksburg,
the ruined American city across
the Rappahannock River. For three days,
Walt searched for his brother
at field hospitals and surgeries,
until he finally took a train to Falmouth,
where he found George in good spirits.
The brothers talked all night in Dixie.
Whitman stayed, buried soldiers
under the white flag in the democratic
earth, or visited at the "Lacy House"
a Confederate captain, 19, prisoner
from Mississippi, one leg, an affection
he called romantic. This is before
Washington, snow in his beard, and the lilacs.

Rahsaan Roland Kirk at the Village Vanguard

Not even girls made you feel this grown up at 15,
sneaking into the Village Vanguard: the red wine
champagnoise, Wild Duck, too sweet,
making you feel up close to a mountain
of a man trick-fingering skritch, manzello,
and tenor, triple threat, each sax, robust,
just off in its own voice together, out of kilter,
exorcising anything European. Kirk says
too much medicine took his eyes—his nurse
drunk, drugged, or mad at someone. Then
three saxophones came to him in a dream
at the Ohio State School for the Blind.
Years later he'd taunt Miles Davis, in concert
across the island. *See this, Miles, this is how it's done.*
The unclassified man *could hear around corners*
and play "Bright Moments" to raise the dead.

Timepiece

Sometimes history comes together
in one place, like Perecman's
Jewelry Shop out Whalley Avenue,
where Perecman himself still repairs
watches, and since you just
cracked the crystal on yours
you make your pilgrimage there.
When you walk in, some guy,
around sixty, recognizes you,
maybe it was a bar downtown,
maybe it was in Vietnam.
Because nothing rings a bell,
he lets it go and starts complaining
about the neighborhood, and if
anyone should know, it's Perecman,
a last holdout from the exodus.
The only solution is a police state,
but nobody wants that.
You're guessing that this guy
comes in just to chat with the old man.
After his last tour in Vietnam,
he bought a big house
around the corner, the 70s,
which is to say it's worth
nothing now. He says
the other night two women
dressed up on the corner
came over to ask him to party.

It was late, and before he could think,
one grabbed him, and the other
held a knife to his jaw.
They weren't women after all.
"Weren't you afraid?"
You imagine his Saturday night,
his house needing paint,
moons burnt into the grass
by dog piss. He says he carries
a gun now in the breast of his coat
like a dark bird in its nest.
He's shot more people in Vietnam
than he has fingers. I watch
Perecman, nearly eighty,
European, his steady hands,
his gift of good vision,
a jeweler's black eyepiece
and tweezers picking through
boxes filled with golden gears,
spindles, and springs so small
that they seem like the inner
workings of a miniature world—
he's made a living out of
this kind of precision.

Greensboro

A gorgeous day in Greensboro, you're reading
in a large lecture hall to eight people. One
is Mary Jarrell—tall, handsome, and convivial.
Despite the years, you'll always see her with Randall
in that shot of the open sports convertible,
with Mary's daughters, Alleyne and Beatrice,
a large picnic basket between them, Laguna Beach,
Randall in full smile at the high point
of his biography, when he'd already written
of Whitman, *even admiration feels like insolence*
and published the odd book *Pictures,*
the good years, the private tribe of two, yearning
for the insouciant pleasures of the drive
Where everything went by but time.

Aeneas in Houston

Although your father doesn't hold the golden bough
like Aeneas but a fork instead at the Longhorn Café,
you could tell he'd spent too much time in hell,
the bedside of his own father's dying. He needed
a weekend with the living, even in blinding Texas
with his son, where his order comes over easy with grits.
This must be the role of the father, to explain
the facts of death. Even Anchises taught his son
its hierarchy—the ones who come back, the ones
who wander, and the ones who disappear altogether.
How does a son console a small Jewish man
under mounted longhorns, ribbons from a rodeo,
and the Lone Star logo?

Your Lingual Heart

Friday night at the ER,
wires taped to your greased chest.
Is it the labial dental constrictive
of a leaky valve like *veuve*,
the French for widow,
or the flip flop
triple tonguing of CVPs?
Maybe the worse of two murmurs,
one that sounds like *Kentucky*
and the other *Tennessee*?
Whatever it is you promise
to change your life.
You wait on your
stainless steel bed
like being forgotten,
your heart comforts itself
like a child,
Tennessee, Tennessee . . . .
You focus on an image
of the sea to slow the waves
when they break, to pace
your own frantic heart.

The Separation

It isn't Aphrodite but a beauty anyway, just when
you need it at your apartment window: a hummingbird

hovering over a flowering weed growing in
the cracked pavement where the condensation

from the air-conditioner drops down. Nothing turns out
quite the way you expect it. The spirit of good auspices

is smaller than a tree roach under the pygmy leaves
of a live oak. The hummingbird is there

when Aphrodite calls from an impossible distance
and grows quiet on the phone or talks, does dishes,

recounts her son's heroics on a Little League field.
Or sometimes beauty comes on its own

when you are entirely alone, a book in hand,
the page opened up to universal sadness.

The Weather Channel

*Hast thou, spirit, perform'd to point
the tempest I bade thee?*
— Prospero

John announces he wishes
he'd invented The Weather Channel,
the highest ratings during a disaster.
Now Blanco, Henly,
Dripping Springs are under
the radar's deep sweeping green
spotted orange and yellow,
the advisory in bleeps and stars
telling us to avoid windows
and to seek shelter
in closets. Frannie
is buried in terriers on the couch
while counseling Mary on
winter pruning. Erin speaks
to the heavens on her new
pink phone, and her brother Jason
is lost in a thick mystery,
a dead woman nearly naked
on its jacket. The system
is now just west of Austin,
but John bets it will miss us.
The wind stirs the darkening branch
over the house he built with his
own hands, while Ariel, Erin's
little gray kitten, is poised to attack
the draft in the tall white curtain.

The Satellite Dish at La Quinta Inn

You've traveled a long way—
you, your wife, and your wife's dog, Jake—
all the way from Paris to see
your friends in Houston and your family in Austin.
You've made your calls, had your *apéritifs,*
and eaten your Cajun redfish
with sautéed *écrevisses* and Chardonnay.
Now you're out late walking Jake
around a satellite dish planted
among palmettos and pointed at an angle
to the city's western overcast sky,
the orbital path of one satellite
following another. The odor,
like night-blooming jasmine
mixed with petroleum, fuses the night
with the night before your last leaving,
seamless, as if you could say
the parting words all over,
even out here beyond the towers,
the Loop, leash in hand,
steady traffic on the feeder.

Virginia

Your father sets out, as always, alone
on his long trip in the off-season
when the campsites are open
but empty. He can go for weeks,
photographing trees and landscapes
that will keep him busy
through winter in the darkroom.
Even as a kid, you thought of him
as an original, a trapper or an explorer,
everything he needed loaded in the car—
rain gear, pup tent, cameras.
He complains that photography
has dwelt on impact rather than
pattern, how the eye is always pulled
to the human figure. He is sleeping
somewhere on the ground,
and the cards come: New Market,
Skyline, James River. He writes
that after the summer mobs,
the deer draw near, addicted to sugar.

4.

Timepiece

1

I set six brown eggs to boil with cold water
and notice how they cluster at first,

                      almost symmetrical,

a single egg forming the center. With more heat,
they hop on the stainless steel bottom
into a formation of threes like dots on a domino.

I don't know the physics of it, the biophysics,
the stove almost purring with vapor,
fragile shells ticking on metal,

                      the precipitate
of ovalbumin inside the brown shells, stiffening into
a perfect white form, a yellow sphere inside it,
a nucleus denatured on its surface.

2

I never dream of the dead
                but small tasks
like boiling eggs recall them:
my grandmother and the health hazard of her cooking.

But unlike the saying, she *could* boil an egg,
ones you'd cut a cap off, salt and pepper,
the hot yolk, loose inside the white cup, the sun

pouring into an immaculate kitchen—
the trick was the three-minute timer,
flowing white sand I'd watch for hours.

3

The first time I had chlodnik was on West 21st Street,
my aunt's apartment filled with odors
of oil paints, turpentine, and toy poodles

that peed on newspaper under the hot water heater.
My aunt made an unlikely living as an artist
and showing dogs in New York City.

Black hair tied back, bangs down to her eyes,
a pointed chin, and slender neck,
she was more stunning than beautiful.

Between her novels and poetry, she'd hung
a Shunga print, genitals magnified like monsters,
amid patterns on flowing fabric,

leaving me silent over
                    fuchsia in a bowl
with chopped hard-boiled eggs, chives,
and sliced red-rimmed discs of radishes.

4

The older my aunt and grandmother grew
the more Asian they looked—

some genetic echo of the Golden Horde,
the merciless engendering of the conqueror
still there in their faces.

                    The last time
I saw them both, my grandmother,
hard-boiled eggs in her purse,
flew in from Miami.

5

While my grandmother was dying in Florida,
my aunt died in Guadalajara
in a shuttered hotel room
                     following a manic phase.

My grandmother never learned of her daughter's death
or her desperate mission.

 My aunt lost her rent control;
                    virtually homeless,

she planned to draw and paint outside the Mexican city
full of children and chickens.

6

I cannot boil eggs without recalling them
or William Bailey's still lifes,
the eggs placed arbitrarily,
                              but in unlikely balance

of white and brown eggs,
the weight and shape of gray bowls and blue-lined pitchers,

a symmetry so foreign to the chaotic heart
that it becomes timeless.

5.

Carthage

Three boys, Tunisian, no older
than thirteen, stand five feet
from a woman reading under
a blue hotel umbrella.
Clearly, they're trying to
shame her in her personal
shade where she is topless.
They stare at her breasts,
the soft brown circles of her
nipples, a judgmental pose,
aggressive, as if their fathers
stood in their bodies.
She is beautiful, chooses
not to look at them, brushes
the sand from the crease
of her book. The boys,
after all, are trespassing
on this private beach
just beyond the blue boats
looped with nets, small waves
lapping their bows.
The powder-pale sun,
a disc in the coastal haze,
shines on almost no one
all the way to the mound
of Carthage, hardly a column

standing, two ancient ports
where birds wade.
The Romans, in their final
annihilation, salted the soil
to kill the crops:
to believe it you are invited
to taste the earth.

Beginnings

On the ground floor called "Beginnings,"
a fertility stone is displayed
in the diamond-hard blue halogen,
a line etching of an erection
with two equal circles, as one sees
in graffiti in the Underground.
The stone is attributed to the Picts,
named from the Latin *picti*,
painted people, tattooed.
The artifact is set
side by side with Latin engravings
and Roman military hardware.
In the museum, you rise
through time, the text in first
person plural, as if all
who enter are complicitous
with the articles of defiance,
from Robert the Bruce, the long
unveering heredity of defeat,
the room of thumbscrews
and "The Maiden" for severing
heretical heads of witches,
upward to the Reformation,
then the rout of the Highlanders
and the exile of the Bonnie Prince,
the museum a deep well
where the fertility stone

of the painted people
rests at the bottom,
universal hieroglyph
on which someone made a wish.

An Untruth

When I enter the stables,
a swallow clips my chest
with its wing in such a rush
to escape her corner over
the musty feeding trough.
She finds a nearby wire
and scolds me. My intrusion
brings back an enduring
untruth, never wholly
amended from what one kid
tells another—that swallows
will go for your eyes
when nesting. It's a small lie,
compared to the Shroud of Turin
or that older women
will burn you if you
make love to them.
In the moment that we touch,
veering swallow, startled man,
at the threshold of daylight
and inner dark, I admit
I see Jocasta's brooch
and Oedipus,
the self-punishing hand.

Vengeance

Surely sex is the only vengeance we get
against desire, feeling the tick
of someone's pleasure just inches
from our thoughts, like saying
something perfectly true
that there are no words for
through untucking, undoing,
and open tender aggression,
why begging *because*, because
the true thing craves saying again.

The Mole

When you go down,
you rule the underworld,
endowed with strange
powers of sense
and black hemoglobin
to keep your breath,
muscles to channel
clay under humus
and flowerbeds to the roots
below the planetary
parts of a garden.
You are a clawed carnivore
of wriggling things,
though made like
the softest parts human,
napped bone and skin.
Here are the damp odors
of summer solstice,
breached solitary walls,
a night breeze
in the upper world
like a ceiling fan
turned low.
You knuckle up
the dark side,
earth-covered shoulders.

No need have you
of sight to mate
a velvet glove.

A Condensed History with Wolves

for Ellen Hinsey

1. *Domestication*

A woman bares her breast
      to a cub and puts a human
   spell on it with human milk.

2. *Capitoline Wolf*

The she-wolf suckled two infants
      that came to her
   drifting on the flooded Tiber

to the foot of the Palatine
      and founded Rome.

3. *Wolves of Paris*

In winter, the invaders
      breached the city walls,
   then unleashed themselves

on the people—
      wolves at the sacred doors
   of the cathedral.

4. *Short Armistice*

They amassed, starving,
      at Kovno, Wilna, Minsk
   where the Prussians and the Imperial Army

littered the battlefield.
    The two enemies joined forces
  to kill wolves.

5. *Ansbach*

Trapped, shot,
    dressed as the burgermeister—
  mask, wig, beard—

the wolf hung from the village gibbet.

6. *Pathetic Fallacy*

Across the bridge of Saint Nicolas
    is the *fontaine du loup.*
  The wolf is prostrate,

one paw across its eyes,
    weeping.

7. *What We Make of Them*

Loup garou, Bête de Gévaudan, shape-shifters,
    chilling human howl—
  a version of ourselves.

8. *Scala Naturae*

If touched, they fall
       on the angelic scale
   to assume false masters.

9. *How They are Hunted*

Dogs track them,
       catch the scent of their evasions,
   fugitives on melting snow,

until they double back, at last,
       on the fallen self.

10. *Wolf of Gubbio*

At Gubbio peace was found,
       the wolf offering Saint Francis
   a paw. This pact was for us

to glean the divine gesture—
       forgiveness,
   the wolf wearing a halo.

Quiet Storm

Christmas lights are still
up in the village
and the canal, at last, is frozen,
the vacation barges raised
in dry dock
though they look as if
they are floating on snow.
And when it is snowing
here is all there is,
a swarming—
school, bridges, and a pharmacy,
its green light and remedies
in a corner of
a large whitened room.
We've said goodbye
to a bad year
as if it were a person
we loved but
couldn't take with us
into this year
with its own stars
but no blacker
and no other lives
to relive,
live, or live after.

Chateau de Chambord

Loire Valley, 1987

My mother occupies her own light
at the lowest aperture
of winter. She is bundled up,

walking Angel, her Golden—
long dead now—from the carriage-house hotel
where we are staying

toward the black trees
where kings of Europe once hunted.
Thin snow blows

from the monolith of a cooling tower
by the wide frozen river.
The chateau is closing, a last

light or two; my mother calling Angel
in the dark by the trees
where only the snow is not natural.

On Marriage

The cello has many secrets
but it never sobs
                    —Zagajewski

Mary took out her cello,
a mummy inside its case,
that stood for years in a nook
beside some bookshelves.
Something she loved
when she lived alone
now resists her. Even the tuning
slips before settling down
to business where
harmonics correspond.
Then through a first attempt
at scales, from the low
to a higher hum, each
fingering missing its mark;
the descent is much closer.
Outside it is almost dark,
June is gone, and a blackbird
whistles in a chestnut,
more melodious than the lower
tones of persistence,
my wife as she was,
not young, but much younger,
before she knew me
and put her cello down.

Last Tiger in Singapore

Victoria ended the 19th century
dying in the first
year of the 20th.
Soon after, the last tiger
in Singapore
was shot in the Billiards Room
of the Raffles Hotel.
The last mouse deer
was gone too,
the last porcupine,
the last clouded leopard.
A century after Victoria,
the day's last rivet
hammers a highrise
at sunset, the last
prayer is sung
at dusk in the mosque,
the last thought
we share about travel
on our last stop home,
the things
we say before sleep,
the last words
I read to you about
the Sri Miramman Temple,
that Tamils still walk

the bed of coals
but are seen
hot-footing the last steps.

6.

Elegy for a Muse

for Laura Strachan

Dina Vierny, d. 1/20/09, was a legendary young model
who inspired the great sculptures and paintings of Maillol's
last years. D.V. also modeled for Matisse, Bonnard, and Dufy.

1

Early autumn storm, the foothills above

> *the spill of rain-rimmed lights,*

a night where death begins

> *in a birthplace, Banyuls on the sea.*

2

Even La Métairie, atelier, beautiful refuge

> *is no refuge, where youth once undressed*

infallible artistic power,

> *where nature makes its effects with almost nothing*

3

surfaces, the nuanced shadow of a muscle,

> *the porous borderlands of being*

turned into monuments.

> *Beauty taken from life is decorative,*

4

but life taken from beauty is difficult—
                    at the end it was Dina,

serene full-form body, "The River"
                    without a bed, limbs flowing, suspended.

5

It takes a long time to find
                    the effects of nature, until they are there,

mastered, lead filled with human weight.
                    I know they are not me, *Dina said sixty years la*

6

But they were and they weren't,
                    even the unmistakable curl of her lip,

the architecture of the round
                    brow and breast, the natural parting of the legs

7

that is legend. What death needs to work with
                    is almost nothing, Maillol

tumbled in a car, chin broken,
                    the slick black road, and the

8

facing of a wall, the last canvas

$\qquad$ *the absence of will—the last image*

that stopped the lit heart, the female form

$\qquad$ *filling the entire frame.*

2009-2010 Books from Pecan Grove Press:

Ahl, Liz. *Luck.* 2010.
ISBN: 978-1-931247-75-7 $7

Aitches, Marian. *Ours Is a Flower.* 2010.
ISBN: 978-1-931247-78-8 $15

Balcárcel, Rebecca. *Palabras in Each Fist.* 2010.
ISBN: 978-931247-60-6 $15

Carbó, Nick. *Chinese, Japanese, What Are These?* 2009.
ISBNJ: 978-1-931247-64-1 $15

Frost, Helen. *as if a dry wind.* 2009.
ISBN: 978-1-931247-66-5 $15

Hall, H. Palmer (editor). POEtry / PrOsE. *2009.*
ISBN: 978-1-931247-68-9 $5

Harper, Cynthia A. *Lipstick.* 2009.
ISBN: 1-931247-73-3 $15

Kemp, Robin. *This Pagan Heaven.* 2009.
ISBN: 978.1.931247-64-1 $8

LaVilla-Havelin, Jim. *Counting.* 2010.
ISBN: 978-1-931247-80-1 $15

Levin, Carol. *Red Rooms and Others.* 2009.
ISBN: 978-1-931247-57-3 $8

Moore, Trey. *Some Will Play the Cello.* 2010.
ISBN: 978-1-931247-70-2. $17

Pettit, Holly. *To One Who Lives on the Mainland.* 2010.
ISBN: 978-1-931247-71-9 $17

Reeves, Phoebe. *The Lobes and Petal of the Inanimate.* 2009.
ISBN: 978-1-931247-65-8 $8

Rojas Joo, Juan Armando. *Rió Vertebral / Vertebral River.*
2009. ISBN: 978-1-931247-60-3 $18

Reeves, Phoebe. *The Lobed and Petals of the Inanimate.*
2009. *ISBN: 978-1-931247-65-8 $7*

Saidi, Mo H. The Color of Faith. 2010.
ISBN: 978-1-931247-79-5. $15.

Witte, Francine. *First Rain.* 2009.
ISBN: 978-1-931247-61-0 $8

For a complete listing of Pecan Grove Press titles,
please visit our website at
http://library.stmarytx.edu/pgpress